Aubrey was born in Georgetown Guyana and immigrated to Canada as a young boy. Aubrey worked with children for a number of years. He worked as a Youth Leader for the City of Toronto's Parks and Recreational Programs and as a Community Youth Leader and mentor at one of Toronto's largest evangelical churches.

Sam & Rita Burke, Aubrey's uncle and aunt were both educators and opened one of Canada's largest African / Caribbean and Multicultural bookstores. That was where Aubrey fell in love with children's literature. Through selling books to schools, childcare centres, teacher conferences, and community events Aubrey's passion for children's literature grew; He was already writing poetry and performing spoken word across North America then fell into storytelling naturally.

"Fly Little Black Bird Fly", was written in 1998 after Aubrey attended his first Harry Jerome Awards. There he was inspired to write a story that would touch, effect, empower and change lives positively.

Aubrey, a man of many talents also wrote the lyrics to the song "Fly Fly Way Up High", that is featured in "Fly Little Blackbird Fly."

He is the President of Envision Urban Media Sales & Marketing where he helps companies plan and buy their media. The other division of his company sells advertising and promotions for several media outlets and events. After consulting with many travel companies Aubrey obtained his Tico license to become a Travel Agent so that he could better serve his clients.

Aubrey believes that there isn't anything that you cannot accomplish if you put your mind to it. Make your passion your living and everything else will fall into place.

He has spoken at the Catholic Children's Aid Society and has inspired students across many School Boards in Ontario, both in Elementary and High Schools. His books are written strategically to positively impact all ages.

"You Were Born A Winner! You Will Achieve, When You Believe!"

~Aubrey Clarke

This is a story of love, courage, compassion, joy and new found hope in Toronto

'© Copyright 2016 by Aubrey Clarke. All right's reserved

Publisher: Envision Urban
Author: Aubrey Clarke
Illustrator: Mary Monette Barbaso-Crall

Permission to reproduce or tansmit in any means, electronic or mechanical including photocopying, recording, or by any information storage and retrieval system, must be obtained in writing from the author Aubrey Clarke.

To order additional copies or to inquire about other books please contact
info@envisionurban.com

Published November 2014
Isbn: 978-0-9877142-7-5 Softcover v2
Printed by C.S.
Isbn: 978-1-988785-03-5 Softcover v3
Printed by I.S. March 2018
Isbn: 978-0-9877142-9-9 Ebook
www.aubreyclarke.com

It's Not Over Until It's Over!

Ms. Blackbird stood over her egg weeping.
Her wing was still broken from the accident but her heart hurt because of the egg that didn't hatch.

Early that week she had experienced the birth of her daughter Joy.

As Joy slept in the nest nearby,
Ms. Blackbird grew weary.
She cupped the egg in her wing and carried it
up the hill to bury it in a secret place.

That night, there was a thunderstorm.

The wind was blowing fiercely and the rain poured down like a waterfall.

The force was so strong that Ms. Blackbird's egg floated out of the secret place, and fell over the cliff right into the eagle's nest.

This is where the journey started for Ms. Blackbird's other egg.

Courage, and his wife Compassion,
had been out hunting that night and battled the storm home.
The weather was horrible so they didn't notice
the tiny egg in their nest.

The next morning Courage was getting ready to go hunting when Compassion said, "Hurry back! I think today will be the day our eaglets hatch!"

"Okay dear. I won't be long," replied Courage.
Courage had only been gone for five minutes when
Compassion felt something moving beneath her.
Compassion laid many eggs in the past but for some reason none of them hatched.

The movement beneath filled her heart with hope.
Compassion jumped up in excitement,
but when she looked down none of her own eggs had hatched.
She moved the leaf aside to see a baby blackbird.

Compassion looked to the sky and asked, "How did I hatch a little blackbird?"

Compassion was hungry. She glared at the little blackbird, licked her beak then opened her mouth wide.

"Yummy, yummy for my tummy," she said.
Just as she did that, Courage came back and yelled, "Wait, look behind you!"

Compassion looked back. The other two eggs had hatched.
She turned to the little blackbird and said,
"I will call you Hope, for surely you have brought us good fortune.
We will adopt you and you will be part of our family."

The two eaglets and Hope grew up in no time.
and had to go through a coming of age ceremony.

The first thing they had to learn was how to dive and
pick their food up.

Hope became a great diver but for some reason she couldn't pick up
the things her brothers could but it didn't stop her from trying.
Hope told herself, "One day I will do it."

The next test was a test of bravery.
Courage said, "You must bring back the fur from the fox's tail and the first one to retrieve it will be considered the bravest."

Hope's brothers both went before her,
but Sly the fox could see them coming and as the brothers dove down,
Sly brought out his big teeth and growled.
Hope's brothers were so scared that they flew back to the nest and hid.

Hope on the other hand pretended to eat the berries next to Sly's den and as he was leaving, she quickly swooped down and grabbed fur from his tail. Sly was very upset that he was outsmarted by a little blackbird.

Hope flew home with fur in beak. Her parents congratulated her for being named the bravest. The brothers couldn't believe their eyes. They were shocked that their tiny sister outwitted the fox.

The last challenge that Courage gave his children was a test of speed. They had to fly around the park and the first one back would be considered the swiftest in their family.

Courage gave them one week to prepare for the race. Tailwind said, "I will sail on the wind and soar across the finish line at the last minute because I am faster than a falcon." Ironbeak said, "I will fly backwards against the wind and still win because I am stronger than a bear." Then they both went back to their nest to play games.

Hope said to herself, "I will practice hard every day until the race."

Hope immediately started her training. She took her time flying around the park. On the first day, she scouted for dangers that might get in her way.

The next day, Hope searched for other routes.

On the third day, Hope sailed on the wind to see how fast she could go.

On the fourth day, she flew against the wind to see if there was an advantage to what Ironbeak had said.

While practising on the fifth day, Hope stumbled across a hidden shortcut. Then she rested on the sixth day to prepare for the race.

All that week Tailwind and Ironbeak laughed at Hope. Tailwind said, "Hope, you have no hope of winning." Then he laughed with a funny high pitched laugh. "Hee! Hee! Ha!! Hee! Hee! Hee! Ha!

Then Ironbeak said, "You are too small and too weak. Look at your tiny wings and beak." Then he laughed with a deep sounding laugh. "Huh! Huh! Ha! Huh! Huh! Huh! Ha!

On the seventh day, it was time for the race.

Courage said, "Ready, set, go!" Tailwind stood there waiting for the wind to start blowing.

Ironbeak also stood there waiting for the wind to start blowing in the other direction.

Hope immediately took off.

In the mean time, Tailwind and Ironbeak were still waiting for the wind to start blowing. Hope flew through the trees, through the bushes and around the hill. At that moment, the wind started blowing where Tailwind and Ironbeak were.

They took off and just after they left, Hope crossed the finish line.
The brothers had lost once more to their tiny sister.

Hope was named the bravest and swiftest but with all these accomplishments something was still missing. Hope began to question her parents and wanted to know why she looked so much different than the rest of her family.

Compassion and Courage told Hope about the day they found her in the nest. Hope was overwhelmed with emotion and wanted to find her birth family. So she flew to the far side of the park in search of answers.

Just as she got to the dark clouds she looked down and saw the most amazing sight.

It was another little blackbird and it looked just like her. Hope looked away for a second and when she looked back the bird had disappeared. Hope had found her joy.

Hope searched for a week to find the little blackbird until finally one day she saw her twirling and swirling through the air.

Hope met her right where the sun shone the brightest and said, "My name is Hope."

But when that little blackbird closed her eyes, Hope got nervous and flew off before finding out her name.

That very night Wizzy the owl had overheard Compassion and Courage talking about helping Hope find her real parents.

Wizzy flew over to the eagle's nest and said, "I come in peace. I heard that you are looking for the little blackbird's parents. I know who the mother is. She thought her egg had died and buried it. I will go and let her know that Hope is alive."

Wizzy told Ms. Blackbird the wonderful news. Ms. Blackbird danced and sang,

♪ I thought all hope was gone. I didn't think I could be strong.
But things changed one day and now I can say,
It's not over until it's over.
It's not done until it's done.
I'll keep hope alive,
Hold my head up high and everything, will be alright.

Hope and Joy were introduced and the families got together regularly.

The bald eagles decided to visit their cousins, the golden eagles. They left Hope behind so she could spend time with Joy and Ms. Blackbird.

One morning, Joy and Hope approached Ms. Blackbird and asked, "What happened to our father?" Ms. Blackbird replied, "I was on my way home to a place called Scarborough when my wing was broken and I haven't been able to get back to him since."

"So there is a chance he could still be alive," said Hope.

Joy and Hope hugged their mother and flew off to tell Motivae the good news.

Hours later, Motivae flew to Ms. Blackbird with a panic in her voice. "Ms. Blackbird, your daughters are in trouble. They went to Scarborough to find their father. I followed them to North York but turned around to get help when I saw the hawks chasing them!"

Ms. Blackbird and Motivae were both crying when Wizzy flew down and said, "What is the matter?" They told Wizzy what had happened.

"It is time to stop crying Ms. Blackbird. You must be strong." said Wizzy "How can I be strong when I can't fly to go and save my girls?" replied Ms. Blackbird. "Where there is a will there is a way." Wizzy responded.

What Motivae said was indeed true. The hawks were hot on Hope and Joy's tails.

Before the girls knew it, a hawk swooped down and grabbed both of them in its talons. Joy screamed, "Help!" Hope said to Joy, "Don't worry sis, we will find a way out of this. After all, I was raised by eagles and it's not over until it's over!"

www.ingramcontent.com/pod-product-compliance
Lightning Source LLC
Chambersburg PA
CBHW040006080526
44586CB00027B/2903